# Advance Praise for
# *War Bonds*

These are poems for our times, necessary and abundant of the fervent call to freedom. Love's body is in our present if we care, if we walk into ourselves as we touch humanity. It is possible to create a new world, it is possible to become who we are — this collection provides the energy, the timbre of our voice and the leap into the spirit waves.

**—Juan Felipe Herrera**, U.S. Poet Laureate Emeritus, National Book Critics Circle Award Winner and author of *Half the World in Light* and *Everyday We Get More Illegal*

In *War Bonds*, Christina Lux confronts readers with the human race's propensity for war mongering, any type –domestic abuse, civil wars, race-based confrontations, religious warfare, global terrorism, and multinational exploitative manipulations. Thoughtful and heartfelt, these poems cast a broad wingspan in time and space, and are about people's ability to survive, regroup, and rebuild after each blood-letting, but the body remembers, and latent traumas flare up at the earliest provocation. *War Bonds* asks us to stop, imagine, and work meaningfully towards a human community bonded by peace, compassion and understanding rather than war-fears.

Lux writes with passion; her words are terse, but poignantly capture the urgency for a peaceful and equitable justice for all peoples on earth. Thoughtfully delightful and provocative, each poem draws you in.

Christina Lux has written a collection that is mesmerizing in the sheer abundance of places torn by war and conflicts but also mesmerizing in the abundance of resilience. Each poem in this collection opens a door to the prevailing times of darkness but also to the times of possibility and reconciliation. These poems must be read over and over again as if we are reading the world anew. An extraordinary collection that celebrates the human spirit under tragedy and hope.

Christina Lux's poems bring a ray of light to the forefront of war, that time "when soil is blood & blood is soil." Her poems bring radical hope in the middle of major-scale conflicts around the world and also the social wars at home, the battles against racism, the losses of Covid-19, and even amidst the struggle she finds the calm of creation, the shelter of poetry…

# War Bonds

FLOWERSONG
PRESS

poetry by

## Christina Lux

FLOWERSONG
PRESS

FlowerSong Press
Copyright © 2024 by Christina Lux
ISBN: 978-1-953447-15-9


Published by FlowerSong Press
in the United States of America.
www.flowersongpress.com


Set in Adobe Garamond Pro

NOTICE: SCHOOLS AND BUSINESSES
FlowerSong Press offers copies of this book at quantity discount with
bulk purchase for educational, business, or sales promotional use. For
information, please email the Publisher at info@flowersongpress.com.

# Acknowledgements

My deep gratitude goes to those who read early drafts of this manuscript and provided feedback: Juan Felipe Herrera, Marjorie Agosín, Yu-Han Chao, Dawn Trook, Charles Payne, and Jaden Lux Ngafeeson. Thanks also to my writing community: Tanya Golash-Boza, Dalia Magaña, Zulema Valdez, Elizabeth McMunn-Tetangco, Camila Alvarez, Randal Jelks, Tanya Hart, L. Ayu Saraswati, DaMaris Hill, Kim McMillon, Ramonu Sanusi, Christa Fraser, and Su Layug. *Beri wo* to colleagues and neighbors who kept me inspired and offered support: Nigel Hatton, Armando Quintero, Irena Polic, Amanda Swain, Kelly Anne Brown, Katharine Henshaw, Leigh Bernacchi, Mary Ukeje-Mba, Omofolabo AjayiSoyinka, MaryEmma Graham, Estela Perez, Teenie Matlock, Fatima Paul, Alicia Rámos-Jordan, Jeff Yoshimi, Ignacio López-Calvo, Asmeret Berhe, Teamrat Ghezzehei, Brandon Wolfe-Hunnicutt, Susan Amussen, and the Noorani, Kinyang, and Mabu families. *Merci* to Sharry Pino, Glenn Fetzer, and Evlyn Gould, who first taught me the most about poetry. Appreciation to Emily Lin and Heather Wagner who offered advice on archival materials and support with scanning photos and documents. Finally, the greatest respect to my grandmother, Nancy Carson, who held onto Edna Cookingham's diary, photos, letters, and papers for so many years and continually inspired us with her life story.

*The following poems were previously published and are reprinted in this book with permission:*

Lux, Christina. "Halley's Comet, 1986." *Consilience*, Issue 9, June 2022.

Lux, Christina. "black n yellow." *Merced County Times*, May 2021.

Lux, Christina. "lost hoops" and "passover palms." *Merced County Times*, April 18, 2020.

Lux, Christina. "the bow." *#NousSommesParis*. London: Eyewear Publishing, 2016.

Lux, Christina. 8 poems: "cosmic claps," "rise," "fighting the wind," "eschscholzia californica," "sound of stones," "after haiyan," "bamboo in a hurricane," and "wingspan." *Feminist Formations: Journal of the National Women's Studies Association.* (Spring 2015).

Lux, Christina. "Peacock-Black." *La Casa de Colores*. La Familia, Segment 2. Curated by U.S. Poet Laureate Juan Felipe Herrera. Library of Congress. Dec. 2015. (remixed with several other poems)

Lux, Christina. "Confianza." *La Casa de Colores*. La Familia, Segment 1. Curated by U.S. Poet Laureate Juan Felipe Herrera. Library of Congress. Nov. 2015. (remixed with several other poems)

Lux, Christina. "skip that stone." *North Dakota Quarterly*, 79.2 (2014).

Lux, Christina. "what can the Miracle Bra do for You?" on "Tell Me More," National Public Radio, April 10, 2013.

Lux, Christina. "weight of water," "cash crop," "St. Luke's," "freedom spins." *A Ritual to Read Together: Poems in Conversation with William Stafford*. Edited by Becca J.R. Lachman. Topeka, KS: Woodley Press, 2013.

Lux, Christina. 1 poem. Kansas Poem of the Week. *150 Kansas Poems*. Edited by Caryn Mirriam-Goldberg. Dec. 16, 2013.

Lux, Christina. 1 poem. *To the Stars Through Difficulties: A Kansas Renga in 150 Voices*. Edited by Caryn Mirriam-Goldberg. Lawrence, KS: Mammoth Publications, 2012.

Lux, Christina. "menu." *Women's Studies Quarterly*, 38: 1&2 (Spring/Summer 2010): 218-220.

# Preface

*War Bonds* is a book of poems about survival in the face of conflict - both domestic and foreign, intimate and public, and about the bonds we forge in those conflicts. The manuscript opens with poems on contemporary conflicts - from Iraq and Afghanistan, to #BlackLivesMatter, the war in Ambazonia and Cameroon, and gang violence in California's Central Valley.

The book then goes back in time 100 years to the archive of a Chicago pianist and painter, my great-great-great aunt Edna Cookingham, who worked with the YMCA in France to entertain the troops at the end of WWI in the midst of the 1918 flu pandemic. As a child, I discovered her small archive in my grandmother's basement – letters, a diary, photographs, and war papers. While Europe may have experienced demobilization and a peace process in 1919, the echoes of that conflict continue to be felt around the world, binding us still – from Ambazonia and Cameroon to the Middle East.

The third section of the book, "know your enemy (better than the NSA)," points to some of the root causes of violence and conflict – from domestic violence and poverty to patriarchy, white supremacy, and colonialism. Part Four, "bodies on the loose," focuses on the body as a site of both trauma and liberation. Part Five, "how to weave the sun," explores how we move forward – bound together – after conflict, violence, terror, or mass trauma.

# table of contents

## know your enemy (better than the NSA)

## bodies on the loose

## how to weave the sun

# War Bonds

c'mon on now,
there is no home front

# weight of water

do you know the weight of water?
carried on the head for a mile?
sprayed by cannons?
scooped to wash the bodies of your dead?

#Cameroon #Afghanistan

# C-RAM fireworks

lined up latrines: so easily toppled
by the leaping sands of Al Asad,
as are we, puffing cigars from lawn chairs,
watching the C-RAM shoot down mortars
on this 4th of July; nearly toppled,
we trace anti-war poems on blackboards,
while our sisters are blown through Brazzaville windows;
so easily toppled as we scream
at the stars southwest of Leavenworth,
where Bales and Manning sleep in their cells.

#Iraq #Afghanistan #Congo #Kansas

# numbers
*for Ric Salinas*


you got numbers for me?
then let's spin some numbers


i knew you before you could count
before your numbers became years


you move with your numbers
like we didn't drink the same water
climb the same trees catch the same stars


you move with your numbers
as if you forgot that my body gives birth
to your infinite numbers


you move with your numbers
but may you never be bound
from the softness we hold here
in these scars left by your numbers


#placas #California

# black n yellow

Black n yellow caution tape,
stretched; superman's embrace.

there's no transubstantiation
for his family's infinite pattern
of morning-leaving-forehead-kisses
can-we-stay-up-longer bedtime hugs.

everyone please take a seat!
in the school of abolition;
lesson 1: our freedom is bound.

#BLM

# trapped in the frame

they came to chop us down
they came axes in hand
they came to tear us apart
we, we remained standing at their sides
they, not knowing that as they cut us down
our arms extended
beyond the page, beyond the frame, beyond the screen
forever raised in victories to come
holding up the whole universe
intersecting beyond their sights
their crossed machetes locked
they, forever trapped in this scene,
cutting us down while we,
we raise our hands in the air,
hearts bound

#Rwanda #SierraLeone #Congo #Cameroon #Ambazonia

# let justice roll down like a river

roll call from Angola to Chowchilla
them bones, them bones, them dry bones
rise now: join, take on full flesh
be filled with the Spirit's breath
let's take that river upstream
let's row: that river is rolling, rolling
over our land, under our feet
ezekiel's wheel is spinning
the wheel sees all:
prosecutor, officer, judge
the wheel spins as we call:
let our people go
let us go

the people have come in from the harvest
from the hills, from the battle
papa, mama: a fire?
why carry all these ashes?
come with me, the time is here
the crows are scattering throughout the sky
but will return, each to a branch, to rest
come, let us go into battle with love

#Louisiana #California #Cameroon #Ambazonia

1919: resurrection dance

# war work

pack the uniform:
one-piece dress, long coat
sailing for France's
hospitals & camps
charged with lifting hearts
of boys who just want to come home

#WWI #1918pandemic

# NATIONAL WAR WORK COUNCIL
### OF THE
### YOUNG MENS CHRISTIAN ASSOCIATIONS OF THE UNITED STATES

August 27, 1918.

My dear Miss Cookingham:-

      Your offer of overseas service in our Entertainment Section has been accepted. We are now hoping to have you sail for France in this, of course, depending upon the length of time it takes for passports to return from Washington (which may be from four to five weeks) and upon the fact that the Government has the right at the last moment to take for its own use any of our reservations on the boats.

      We have filed with the Government the loyalty blanks and reference letters which we received about you, and in order to start the various things which it is necessary for you to do before sailing, I will give you a list of those which you may do at once.

      You will need to have two and one half dozen photographs taken, size 3x3 inches, price not to exceed two dollars and a half for the lot. (These we will reimburse you for later). Some of these you will need to attach to the various papers required in getting ready to sail, and the balance you will need for use abroad.

      Everyone is required to have innoculations for typhoid and para-typhoid (three innoculations are necessary, each a week apart) and to be vaccinated. A medical test is also required. I am enclosing a card which your doctor must sign stating that you have had the medical examination, the innoculations and the vaccination. This card you must show in France.

      You will also need to obtain either your birth certificate or sworn affidavit to the same. (Form of which is enclosed)

      As soon as you have your photographs and either your birth certificate or affidavit for the same, you may make application for

# tiger rag

the boys:
belligerent, tangled up!
reckless, some heroes!
"peppy," going up!
eager, no place like home!
weary: skeleton jangle
discouraged: look at me

to meet them with the right spirit: the game
we'll teach them to ride their tigers again

#WWI #demobilization

PROGRAMME

1. COTILLION _____
   (League of Nations)

2. ONE STEP _____
   (Jesters' Hop)

3. FOX TROT _____

4. WALTZ _____
   (Forever After)

5. ONE STEP _____
   (Gold Bricks')

6. FOX TROT _____
   (Tangled Up)

7. WALTZ _____
   (Look at Me)

8. ONE STEP _____
   (Tickle Toe)

9. FOX TROT _____
   (Going Up)

10. WALTZ _____
    (Long Absence)

11. ONE STEP _____
    (Some Heroes)

12. FOX TROT _____
    (Flat Foot)

13. ONE STEP _____
    (Asthma)

14. WALTZ _____
    (No place like Home)

EXTRAS

WALTZ
(Bon-Bon)

ONE STEP      WALTZ
(I Hope)   (Check Up)

-oO**Oo-

# resurrection dance

from shouldered rifle
to hand on her shoulder blade
from marching in step
to gliding across the floor
from a stiff salute
to her light hand on his arm
a foxtrot, a waltz:
a body reborn

#WWI #demobilization

A P R I L   F O O L   D A N C E

Given for

THE ENLISTED PERSONNEL

BASE HOSPITAL ONE HUNDRED ONE

Tuesday Evening, 1st April 1919.
8:00  P. M.

AMERICAN RED CROSS RECREATION HUT
ST NAZAIRE                    FRANCE

18

# pauline, pauline

pillbox like a mouth:
Gertrude says Pauline
was how they named that machine

Pauline, Pauline,
please just let it be:
an orchard, rows of trees

#WWI #GertrudeStein #Aisne #Soissons

# tips from a red cross driver
*after Robert W. Service's "A Casualty"*

when soil is blood
& blood is soil

take the bumps slow:
easing the pain
of both driver
& almost slain

tell each other it's all ok:
even the fresh-turned earth knows
it's not so much a lie
as a last sweet offering

#WWI

**know your enemy
(better than the NSA)**

*"All tragedy
is first
family tragedy."*

—*Abdourahman Waberi*

# boy, walking in rain

Terror is teaching my child
"No hoodie in the rain"
Terror is telling my boy
"Don't play tag in the yard"
Terror is taking my son.

Terror has come out to play…
Terror's been roaming our streets….
Terror's got the law and a gun.

My people, my people:
Why are we standing alone here,
Mother and Son,
in front of that law and that gun?

#TrayvonMartin #TamirRice #BLM

## menu

mahogany diet coke
GUESS chain carnations
French stab green beans
chop chop chop chop

their cackle cadence
me rappelle
hup hup hup

my one brother
*Tae Guk Gi*
onyi
<when can i come home>

could you turn it down
>just a little<
the war is getting old
bumi baby bumi

slatted chaise marronne
corner tableau: cyclone
alarme au feu
sortie

red drinks, pearl strings
dos à dos: fourchette / couteau
bracelet amitié: 1993


star spangled
credit
Visa
debit

mon petit frère s'en va-t-en guerre

#Iraq

## TRANSLATIONS:

me rappelle – reminds me
*Tae Guk Gi* – Korean film, released as *The Brotherhood of War* in the U.S.
onyi – big sister
bumi – sleep
chaise – chair
marron - brown
tableau – painting
cyclone – cyclone
alarme au feu – fire alarm
sortie – exit
dos à dos – back to back
fouchette - fork
couteau -  knife
amitié – friendship
mon petit frère s'en va-t-en guerre – my little brother's going to war

# domestic peace

"They let him go free?"
My son dropped all he was holding,
laid flat on his back, mouth open,
no interest in the President;
news anchors; live feeds; aftermath.
later, he just asked,
"Will that police officer get his job back?"
and, eyes wide,
"What if he does it again?"

#MichaelBrown #BLM

# this August 9th

a wild-bearded white man
ran down the street,
into traffic, my lane

The man just ran
The man was never stopped
He was not shot
He never laid in the street.
He ran, free.

Over dinner you guess
He lost his wife
His daughter or his son
And broken, ran

Never thinking of the boy
Shot walking down the street
One year ago this day.

#MichaelBrown #BLM

## cascara

we plucked red cherries,
dropped into baskets
balanced on our heads
to the mango tree
where we turned ripe flesh

to pulp, revealing white seeds
spread out on grass mats
next to ma's concrete tombstone
dried in the noon sun

as we chased the goats away,
never imagining you
would not know coffee is red,
sweet, round, carried on children's heads

#NWCameroon #Ambazonia

# a little cash crop in your cup?

coffee: never bitter at 9,
sweet red beans plucked and sampled;
its aftertaste came at 15,
learning the meaning of famine
& cash crop in a day.

#NWCameroon #Ambazonia

# take me to the water

Hike with me to the top of the hill,
Stretch your body across the catchment.

Never let your water lie
In the hands of a gas can,
A tool, a payment, a tap,
A pipe, a tank, Associations.

Let it rest in children's mouths,
Flow over each small body,
Instead of being carried
For miles each day on their heads.

#NWCameroon #Ambazonia

# bamboo in a hurricane

novels: my shield at 12
(yes, the "marrying age")
clasped on a bamboo bed
fend off the world of men
by hurricane lamplight

#NWCameroon #Ambazonia

# calabash

Intricate carved mahogany screen
hides matching turquoise Moroccan plates,
black pyrographed ochre calabash,
all in pieces and shards on the floor
I refused to sweep up, mop up, die.

Now taro watches we three,
sharing notebooks, paper, pen,
Creating here in the sun:
Futures, beyond a quick fix.

# expertly trained

to be blank
eyes
to be open
mouthed
to be flawless
to be ready
to receive
all you sell
to convince me
i can be
naturally
perfect

# sound of stones
*after Flora M'mbugu-Schelling's "These Hands"*

do you know the sound of stones
hammered till dusk in the quarry?
cast by the sinless?
yielding blooms before leaves?

#Mozambique #Tanzania

**bodies on the loose**

*"Love is a battle, love is a war, love is a growing up."*

*—James Baldwin*

# Bodies in the Street

Nature herself protests:
Wind and trees move as one
Soil gives way to rising roots
Upended oaks and palms
Lay their bodies in the street
As if to say, how can you
go to school on such a day?

#J20 #DC #Bamenda

# eschscholzia californica

native to both nations,
self-seeding,
drought-resistant,
she blows freely
across the border.

#California

# wilder

it's getting wilder out here:
we're accompanied by
a convoy of dragonflies
tens of calves on every side
coyotes howling, it's time...

#2020U.S.election #COVID

# wingspan

*para Alicia*

do you know the wingspan of poems?
soaring across the border?
smashing the bits in our mouths?
so our tongues may stutter, skipping
through languages
to build the beat of radical love?

# lemon & salt

scrubbing the coffee pot
with lemon and salt

brings me back
to waiting tables
at Chuck's diner

we servers all knew:
what cleanses glass
stings open wounds

# sting, butterfly

more? let's go
1-1-2-1-2
your shoulders bounce light
comet clusters
refracted by scars
that taught you
always
bend those knees
on them hooks

# red dew

red dew petals prick
soft flesh: liquid blooms glisten
thorn-drawn second life

# what can the MiracleBra do for *you*?

propped on white sheets
MiracleBra tossed
on a vacant chair
scanning the pamphlet
"Your Breast, Our Surgeon"
like I'm not scared

# passover palms

Friday night on our back porch
we face double palms reaching high,
bamboo almost taking over.

my own open palms reflect
a settling in to quarantine;
my man's wide shoulders carry me
through these never empty streets.

the laughter of our kids floats
from Santa Clara through the phone,
no longer in the house at 9.

train horns keep getting louder,
echoed by ambulances;
colors seem strangely brighter.

yet our roses continue
to blossom after this last rain
that seemed more like a great flood.

#COVID19 #California

# lost hoops

then they took down the hoops
the numbers been rising, graphs spiking:
but what knocked the breath out of me - hard,
like I fell off the parallel bars,
was when they took down the hoops.

#NYC #COVID19

# how to weave the sun

*"And we will no longer need*
*Lightning*
*To weave*
*Suns"*

—*Véronique Tadjo*

# COVID summers

Green hills of lush grass
Turn golden through our valley -
Wave us back to life

## calm in creation

there is a calm in
creation

there is a peace in
pruning the roses
picking tangerines
watching the lemons ripen

there is a comfort in
your thigh
pressed into mine
new, familiar
and old

# water people

water people know the secret
of flow the fire
the undertow
of natural rhythms
why we lose time on the dance floor

# skip that stone

skip that stone across the lake again
tell me: the shape, the speed don't matter
it's all in the angle, the angle
as it cuts the water

# no more tension on the line

a single duck's wake
my slack line: sinking, rising
cross sky on the lake

seagull circles my bobber
swoops over cirrus-water
dives to steal my fish!

spit out the hook
in the shallows – no more
tension on the line

## water safe

at 6, we learn
to float,
bellies up,
noses dry,
holding hands,
counting stars,
knowing better
than to reach up
& catch them
lest we sink.

# merced means mercy

two blue birds or three
jumping from tree to tree
talk to each other through the fog

# At the Cinema Cafe

Two blood orange mariposas float,
starched tablecloths nearly take wing,
a pair of pigeons flash pink throats...
even these umbrellas may lift off
as we sit perched on the sidewalk
hoping to learn to fly

# prophecy

four little geckos
sing on the wall
to a chorus of crickets

# fighting the wind

I have seen you
fighting the wind!
they see only windmills;
what greater love
risks insanity
for a sister's justice?

# rise

have you heard the crickets
calling, calling your names,
waiting for you to rise
faster than a grove of bamboo?

# confianza

He backs us up with a martial beat
He backs us up on the street

Then pulls our chins to the sky
With a one off reminder
To always step off the line.

My son prophesies in portraits:
"The man of the future protects."

# #porteouverte

these streets we hold
as doors open,
cross nine bridges
in one deep breath

#Paris2015

# date palm

the fronds look like knives
until you notice they bend
in the wind more like fingers
reaching down: so many hands
extended to cover us.

#Merced2015

# threshold

we are the threshold
to the moonbow
we are the light
bouncing off the moon
we refract all color
as water crashes
we abide; span worlds:
a most delicate arch,
from Yosemite to Kauai
from Plivice to Victoria
we stretch, born of night

#Orlando2015

# the bow

the two child prophets
rebuild the world from laughter
slide right down Noah's old bow,
sail above troubled waters
then over Rome: hands floating
then clasped, all moons at their feet,
clothed in sun, shining, no words
k'auna, amore sans fin

#Maiduguri #Merced #Paris #Orlando

## supernova

When my heart burst
like a supernova,
I chose to leave a piece
with you and you and you.

From that fragment
a universe will be born
as your eyes flash one day,
as you stop yourself
from shattering another world,
or reach out to take a child's hand,
or stay with her when you want to go.

From the remnant of my heart
will be born new stars, new worlds.

# look up! look up!

hundreds of birds
circle outside our windows
as if to say
look up! look up!

# cosmic claps
*pour Fatima*

she spins like the sun,
gathering us in;
her laughter, a solar wind,
releases aurorae,
generating cosmic claps

# freedom spins

"Mama, how can I be your Freedom?
And did you know you are my Freedom?"
At 6, he grins & skips & spins
As I learn his radiant lexicon

# peacock-black

his eyes,
shut tightly,
like oysters
open in a flash:
South Sea
peacock-black,
refracting all color
to the world

# after haiyan

la leche, the milk, will come in
we see you pumping pumping
breathing for your children
at the altar
night & day!

#Philippines

## catch

we are catching poems
harnessing that wind
to create shelter

#haiyan #Philippines

# halley's comet, 1986

were you watching too as she flew?
from the barbed wire fence along the canal?
could you catch her solar-wind-tail?
did you know she spins in reverse?
did you spy her rainfire of shooting stars?
did the sonic boom echo from our shell?

they say we can tell a star's age
by how fast it spins.

could we spin until she passes again,
binary stars born of a great collapse,
orbiting one center of mass?

## armor

each day we choose
between amor and armor
all ten of us

spreading masa on corn husks
repairing the broken ones
placing the single olive

waiting the long steaming hours
until they're plucked
like fruit, ripe, whole

ready to be peeled open

# foothills

did you know?
i'm waiting to see you
come over that hill

did you know?
i'm waiting to see you
run over that hill

did you know?
i'm waiting to see you
jump over that hill

did you know?
i'm waiting to see you
fly over that hill

did you know?
i'm waiting to see you
again.

# you brought the rain

i have been waiting to watch you play.
i'm waiting to watch you play.
i would love to watch you play.
come please, play.

lo siento
pardonne-moi
je t'ai perdu
pour la dernière fois.

i have been waiting (for 20 years)
to watch you play.
i am waiting (here, in our homeland)
to watch you play.
i would love (now, in this moment)
to watch you play.
come please, play.

lo siento
perdóname
te perdí
por última vez.

i called to you
across the desert
and you, you brought the rain,
       you brought the rain,
         you brought the rain.

# brazzaville tide

The people come in waves…
do you feel their undertow?
The Sun-Moon witness builds the tide,
The pattern, the deep pulse
Of waves that rise up and crash
again and again and again.

# communion

Sitting on the stoop drinking
pinot from lawn chairs watching
the traffic just after dusk

Laying on the hotplex roof
wondering if the stars will
remain suspended for us

Heads together, bodies spread,
an A on a grassy hill,
high on sweet rotting mango

Searching for passion fruit we
break open: sucking the smooth
tart seeds like it's our last time

# climbing lessons

be one with the rock
the best partner
is the one that holds you
rest on its face
but know when to leap

## seven of hearts

i believe in a king
that rolls in astride a tank
with a seven of hearts
bursting from its cannon.

i believe we can all be
kings, queens, princes, even
jokers floating in a pool,
held up by a simple faith
in buoyancy, vowing:
even when a prince forgets,
we will never let him sink,
raising him up between us.

# el cap

take me to the base of el cap
where we'll strike a half-moon pose
breathing in the sky
breathing out seventy-seven waves of light

# 10 Mile Run

Give me a
10 mile run
through laughter
soft as fleece
lapis-bright

ending on the beach
with my body arched
in a bow
opened chest
bursting sequoia
sweat beading like dew

# Our Favorite Numbers

He says: zero, the cipher
The most beautiful baseline
From which we measure the world.
Yes, the simplest number,
It adds to nothing: empty.

I'm drowning in sevens;
Stacked, spreading,
Seven hills,
Seven seas,
Seven mountains,
Seven years till jubilee.

We meet at Jericho,
where seven becomes zero.

# yellowjackets

yellowjackets on the pier
dance to banda: float
on the wind across the lake

les abeilles sur le quai
dansent à la banda
flottant à travers le lac

las abejas en el muelle
bailan banda
flotando por el lago

# ask the sun

it'll be ok:
ask the sunshine
carrying our ancestral music
the breath of community liberation

# crossing over

May we carry you in our arms?
Across the desert, the river,
To a wide-open meadow
Where only deer jump,
Where only shooting stars guard us,
Where we breathe in sequoia
As we cross over, brave warriors,
          Into morning?

# B-52s

those B-52s
rumbling, flying low
over barbed wire fence?
have got nothing on your voice

# lost and found

baby you've got me
like the sky's got stars
like fire's got flames
like Zion's got game
like God's got names

# snowpack

your gaze
could melt
the Sierra snowpack
in half a second

# give me one word

one word: magma, hot & slow
one word: thunder, resounding through earth's core
one word: sonic boom, smashing barriers
one word: tsunami, rising
one word: supernova, outshining suns
one word: bold like a lion with its pride
one word: cornerstone, chosen

# witness

our children's laughter mingles
like rivers at the headwaters
leaping across pain and time

light as a bee as it lands
on the top branch of a palm
heavy enough to topple
the whole damn thing

our children's laughter mingles
brushing each wound, bruise, scar, thorn
capable of toppling
the very scaffolding of fear
we grown folks erect each day

our children's laughter mingles,
runs to the ends of the earth,
returning just before dusk
to witness me lean against you
in the sun

# slackline

she always practiced
balancing one foot
while placing the next

on the taut slackline
stretched across the yard
didn't hesitate

to dare to walk
on air

# 安 心 : calm heart

Courage: holding to
     Oír first
     Oír second
     Oír third

Holding: courage to
     Saber here
     Ver now
     Decidir when

El valor de abrazar:
     Speak in open space
     Quiet, warm, alert:
     In power

Of new home futures.

# About the Author

Christina Lux grew up in Planada, California before moving to Texas, followed by Québec and then Cameroon, finally returning to the U.S. for university studies. Her poetry has appeared on National Public Radio, in the Houston Chronicle, and in textbooks by Oxford University Press, as well as in numerous books, journals, and magazines, including *Women's Studies Quarterly* and *Feminist Formations*. She holds a Ph.D. in Romance Languages from the University of Oregon, a Certificate in Conflict Resolution from Cornell University, and Certificates in Conflict Analysis, Negotiation, and Mediating Violent Conflict from the United States Institute of Peace. She previously served as a short-term Cultural Envoy to Brazzaville where she conducted creative writing workshops with youth who had survived the civil war. She is currently Managing Director of the Center for the Humanities at the University of California, Merced.

FLOWERSONG
PRESS

**FlowerSong Press nurtures essential verse from, about, and throughout the borderlands. Literary. Lyrical. Boundless.**

Sign up for announcements about
new and upcoming titles at:

www.flowersongpress.com

Printed in the USA
CPSIA information can be obtained
at www.ICGtesting.com
LVHW031140230224
772606LV00047B/995

*Praise for*
# War Bonds

These are poems for our times, necessary and abundant of the fervent call to freedom. Love's body is in our present if we care, if we walk into ourselves as we touch humanity. It is possible to create a new world, it is possible to become who we are — this collection provides the energy, the timbre of our voice and the leap into the spirit waves.

- Juan Felipe Herrera, U.S. Poet Laureate Emeritus, National Book Critics Circle Award Winner and author of *Half the World in Light* and *Everyday We Get More Illegal*

In *War Bonds*, Christina Lux confronts readers with the human race's propensity for war mongering, any type — domestic abuse, civil wars, race-based confrontations, religious warfare, global terrorism, and multinational exploitative manipulations. Thoughtful and heartfelt, these poems cast a broad wingspan in time and space, and are about people's ability to survive, regroup, and rebuild after each blood-letting, but the body remembers, and latent traumas flare up at the earliest provocation. *War Bonds* asks us to stop, imagine, and work meaningfully towards a human community bonded by peace, compassion and understanding rather than war-fears. Lux writes with passion; her words are terse, but poignantly capture the urgency for a peaceful and equitable justice for all peoples on earth. Thoughtfully delightful and provocative, each poem draws you in.

- Omofolabo AjayiSoyinka, Professor Emerita of Women, Gender and Sexuality Studies and Theatre at the University of Kansas, choreographer, and author of *Yoruba Dance*

ISBN 978-1-953447-15-9

9 781953 447159

FLOWERSONG
PRESS